Supermarine
SPITFIRE

by
The Aeronautical Staff of Aero Publishers, Inc.
in Cooperation with

Edward T. Maloney, Curator of The Air Museum

Scale Drawings by Uwe Feist

Aero Publishers, Inc.

329 Aviation Road
Fallbrook, California 92028

© **AERO PUBLISHERS, INC.**

1966

Library of Congress Catalog Card Number

66 - 22653

IS BN –0 –81 68 –0536 –9

Printed and Published in the United States of America by Aero Publishers, Inc.

THE SUPERMARINE SPITFIRE

By Edward T. Maloney

This is the story about one of the world's most efficient fighter planes of World War II.

From its conception by the famous British designer R. J. Mitchell, to the time in 1947 when the last Spitfire was made, the immortal Spitfire served to carry on a fine tradition.

The Spitfire first flew in the peaceful blue skies of England in 1936. When war clouds loomed on the horizon and finally broke—the Spitfire was among the first to engage the German raiders. They first saw action over the Firth of Forth and later achieved immortal fame during "The Battle of Britain."

The origin and achievement of the Spitfire design lies in the story of the Schneider Trophy Race. After Great Britain had regained the trophy held at Naples, Italy in 1922, the design staff at the Supermarine Works knew a new aircraft of advanced design would be needed to win the next contest.

Reginald Mitchell was at that time chief designer of Supermarine, and from his drawing board came the predecessors of the Spitfire: The S-4, S-5, S-6 and S-6b Schneider Racing Planes.

Their story is well known, and so it need not be repeated here.

In 1931 Britain retired the Schneider Trophy for the third and last time. Speeds in excess of 400 miles per hour had been achieved with Mitchell's S6-b Schneider Seaplane Racer. Air Ministry officials were quick to realize that a new design of the most up to date fighter must be produced if Britain was to hold and retain this record.

Early in 1934, the Air Ministry issued specification F 5/34—calling for a new fighter design carrying eight machine guns.

The Rolls Royce Company brought out a new 12 cylinder liquid cooled engine. Mitchell knew that this was the engine he had been waiting for, and so he completely redesigned his new projected fighter around this new engine.

The idea was well received by the Air Ministry and a new specification number was assigned, F 37/34, to the new aircraft. The number F 36/34 was assigned to Hawkers new aircraft design which became the famous "Hurricane," and flew side by side with the Spitfire during "The Battle Of Britain."

Years later when the skies were filled with fighter and bomber aircraft, even the common housewife could pick out the Spitfire fighters overhead by their beautiful elliptical wings.

It was believed for sometime that the elliptical wing was more efficient than the common straight taper platform type. Production difficulties were overcome by the Supermarine design staff, and the elliptical wing became a Spitfire trademark. This wingshape was used throughout the war, until the introduction of the Supermarine Spiteful.

The Spitfire came into being direct from the drawing boards. A full size wood mock up was made from which a prototype had been ordered.

In March 1936, the Spitfire prototype K 5054 was ready. It was the first modern all metal fighter designed and built in Great Britain.

On March 5th, 1936 Vickers Chief Test Pilot — Mr. Summers — climbed into the cockpit and started the Rolls Royce "Merlin" engine. As Summers opened the throttle the little Spitfire danced and finally shot into the air, after an unbelievably short take off run on the green turf.

Test pilot Summers described the first flight as very delightful. In June 1936 the Air Ministry awarded a contract for 450 Spitfires.

At this time the war in Spain had influenced air power in Europe and British observers knew and reported the Luftwaffe strength in the "Legion Condor."

R. J. Mitchell never lived to see the famous exploits his Spitfire design achieved, for he died in 1937 at the early age of 42 years. He left behind the finest memorial any man could wish for. He had created a design that was to be one of the world's most beautiful fighter aircraft—the immortal Spitfire.

R.A.F. Sq. No. 17 was the first squadron to be equipped with the Spitfire MK-1 and the popularity of the Spitfire grew and grew. The Spitfire made its first public appearance at the dedication of the new Cambridge Airport. Later they became a very common sight when two complete squadrons were stationed at Duxford Air Station.

In the early war years the Luftwaffe swept the skies of Polish, French, and Belgium fighter aircraft. The French Morane, Bloch, and Curtiss fighters were no match for the speedy Messerschmitt Me 109E. The Spitfire was the only answer, and it took up the challenge with relentless attacks on the Luftwaffe attackers.

The prototype Spitfire was an aerodynamically clean aircraft, without any bumps or drag producing lines.

When the Spitfire MK-1 was put into production some of the cleanness had to give way in the interests of mass production and operational efficiency.

The first MK-1's went into service in 1938 and they had a fixed pitch wood propeller. Later an all metal propeller was fitted.

During the first year of the war the experience gained in combat with the Spitfire enabled it to be improved upon. These improvements were embodied into the Spitfire MK. II. A constant speed propeller was fitted to improve rapid climb and increase the service ceiling. This increase in superiority gave an advantage to the Spitfire over opposing German fighters during the "Battle of Britain."

The successes of the Spitfire during the "Battle of Britain" is well known. The Spitfires attacked the high flying Messerschmitts, while the Hurricanes attacked the bombers.

As the war moved forward, later Spitfire models appeared on the scene. The early Spitfire's MK. I and II were returned to training status and were replaced by Spitfire V's. More Spitfire V's were built than any other version. The Mark V was the first Spitfire to be tropicalized. One hundred Mark V Spitfires were loaned to the Royal Navy. And three hundred were shipped to the Royal Australian Air Force for duty in the South Pacific against the Japanese Air Force.

The Spitfire MK. VI was a special high altitude model. A pressurized cockpit was fitted, and it was powered by a Rolls Royce 47 or 49 Merlin engine.

The Spitfire MK. VII was a limited production high altitude fighter. It was later used for meteorological duties.

The Mark VIII was a projected Spitfire trainer project, however the need for operational fighters by the R.A.F. prevented this trainer from being built. A few were modified into two place trainers after the Second World War.

The Spitfire MK. IX was the second largest production model built. It was the Royal Air Force's answer to the German Focke-Wulf FW-190A. This model Spitfire had superior high altitude performance. This was achieved by installing a new 1600 h.p. Merlin 61 engine with a two stage, two speed supercharger.

The Mark X Spitfire was produced for photographic reconnaissance duties. The cockpit was pressurized and extra fuel tanks were fitted in the wing leading edge.

The Mark XI. Spitfire was the mainstay of the Coastal Command photo-recon units. It took part in some of the most important photographic missions ever made over German territory during World War II.

The Spitfire MK. XII was built as a low altitude fighter to combat attacking Fock-Wulf 190's which had been converted into deadly low level fighter bombers. It was the first Spitfire to be fitted with a Griffon engine of 2000 h.p.

Two R.A.F. Squadrons were quickly formed with Spitfire MK. XII's working alongside the new Hawker Typhoon. They were sufficient to stop the troublesome FW-190 raids in the south of England.

It also proved the possibilities of this new Griffon engine for more advanced models in the development of the Spitfire.

The Spitfire MK. XIII was built for low level photo-recon use. Two vertical and one oblique F.24 cameras were used. No cannon armament was carried, however four machine guns were fitted.

The Spitfire MK. XIV was designed as a maximum performance high altitude fighter and a refinement over the earlier Spitfire MK. XII.

The MK. XIV had a lengthened nose to accommodate the 2,050 h.p. Griffon 65 engine. Great attention was paid to the surface finish, and the clean lines of the cowl were again refined to decrease drag to a minimum.

The earlier models were all tropicalized, and the later models built had bubble canopies fitted. These were known as Spitfire MK.XIVE, and they introduced a new armament of two 20 m.m. cannon and two 50 cal. machine guns. A fighter recon model was built, and this carried one oblique F.24 camera and complete armament plus a 33 gallon fuel tank, mounted in the rear fuselage for increased range.

R.A.F. pilots who flew the MK.XIV commented that this model was a fast, nice handling fighter, but that it did not fly like the earlier model Spitfires. This is understandable as the directional rotation of the Griffon engine was opposite to that of the earlier Merlin series engines.

There were no Spitfire MK. XV or XVII. These numbers were reserved, but were later used in the Seafire Series.

The Spitfire MK. XVI went into R.A.F. service in 1944. It was a standard MK. IX airframe fitted with an American built Packard Merlin engine. Later models were fitted with bubble canopies.

The MK. XVIII was a basic MK. XIV with increased range and strengthened wings. They were built in two versions: One was used for interception duties and the other version was used for fighter-recon missions being fitted with cameras in addition to armament.

The MK. XIX was a high altitude photo-recon Spitfire devoid of all armament. After the 23rd model all subsequent aircraft were tropicalised and had pressurized cockpits. Increased fuel tanks were also carried. This was the last photo-recon model in the Spitfire Series. It was powered by a Griffon 65 engine and used a five blade Rotol propeller.

The Spitfire MK. XX was the first experimental model to be fitted with the new Griffon II B engine. Only a prototype model was built, but experience gained from it contributed greatly to the MK. F.21 and MK. F.22 Spitfires which were the final models in the series.

The Spitfire MK. F.21 and MK. F.22 marked the peak of Spitfire design and were the end of the line in the Spitfire series. These two models were in production when VE-Day came in April 1945.

The Wing had been strengthened and completely redesigned, greater range built in, and a Griffon engine fitted. The only difference between the two models: the MK. F.22 had a 24 volt electrical system instead of a 12 volt system and a bubble canopy was fitted for better visibility. One was fitted with a Griffon 85 engine driving a six-blade counter rotating propeller as an experiment.

The long line of Spitfires had gone through extensive alterations. However, they were still Spitfires in shape and form, and they all flew with easy handling forces which made them all popular with the pilots who flew this aircraft.

A total of 20,351 Spitfires were built.

We gratefully acknowledge the photographic assistance of the following persons and organizations:
U.S. Air Force
Tom Piedmonte
Rev. Boardman Reed
Mitch Mayborn
Jim Harvey
Ted Hooton
Steve Caruso
George Gosney
Col. G. B. Jarrett
John Hopten
Royal Air Force
Royal Canadian Air Force
R.A.F. Station Colerne
R.A.F. Station Coltishall
Flt. Off. R. H. Coleman
Wing Cdr. K. Lister
Bill Swisher

A memorial to the ages. This Spitfire Mk. XVI E of Royal Air Force 603 Squadron was formerly Air Vice Marshall Baker's personal aircraft. It was originally coded RW 893.

This view of Spitfire Mk. XVI TE-476 shows the beautiful elliptical wing of R. J. Mitchell's immortal Spitfire. This aircraft was only recently retired from flying the annual Battle of Britain anniversary fly over.

This Spitfire Mk. Vb AB-910 was built in 1941 and first delivered to R.A.F. 222 Squadron. Later it was delivered to 43rd. Group and while there was damaged by enemy action. During 1945 an odd event occurred with this aircraft while it was stationed at Hubbleleston with the 53rd. Operational Training Unit: This was the actual aircraft which took off accidentally with a W.A.A.F. clinging to the tail. The pilot reported tail heaviness but landed the aircraft safely.

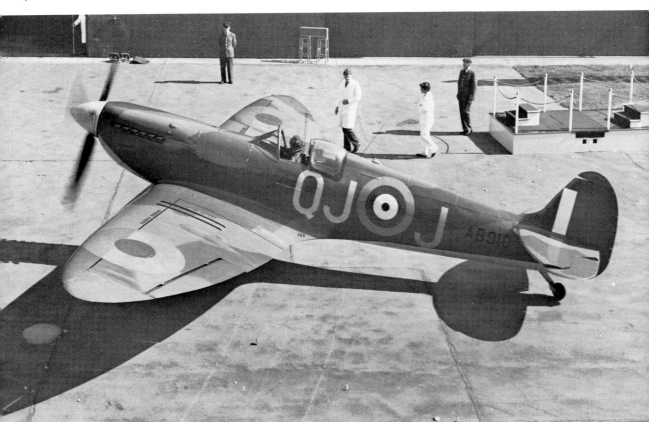

This Spitfire P.R. 19 PM-631 was originally used by the Meteorlogical Flight at R.A.F. Station Woodvale from 1945 to late 1959. The P.R. 19 was a very fast, unarmed photo-recon. aircraft, powered by a Rolls Royce "Griffon" engine. It is seen here on display at R.A.F. Station Coltishall.

This Australian Spitfire Mk. VIII MV-154 is seen at Bankstown Airport, N.S.W. Territory as it appears today. This model was tropicalized for service in South Pacific. The Royal Australian Air Force used a large number of these Spitfire Mk. VIII's during the Second World War.

This Spitfire Mk. IX is one of the few Spitfire aircraft flying in the United States today. Note the different rudder shape of the Mk. IX from the Mk. VIII. Also note the difference in the Merlin engine exhaust stacks.

This view shows the clip wing Spitfire Mk. IX. This aircraft was a former Belgium Spitfire OO-ARF and registered to the firm of C.O.G.E.A. It was used for tow target duties.

Rear view of Spitfire Mk. IX shows small clean lines of the plane. This aircraft is owned by the well known actor Cliff Robertson. It was imported to the U.S. after appearing in the motion picture "The Longest Day".

Unusual view of Spitfire Mk. IX's windscreen, canopy, and cockpit.

The Spitfire Mk. IX featured a four bladed wood propeller by Rotol. The Merlin engine is contained in a neatly cowled, low-drag cowling.

Close up view of Spitfire Mk. IX's Merlin 61 engine and four blade Rotol propeller. Note the six small engine exhaust stacks, and the smooth low-drag cowl fasteners.

Close up detail of Rolls Royce down draft carburetor air scoop reveals clean contour lines.

The success of the Spitfire in aerial combat was largely due to its renowned powerplant—the powerful Rolls Royce Merlin engine.

Spitfire Mk. XVI fuselage featured a simple light weight but sturdy structure.

Interesting view of Spitfire's engine mount. Basic structure of Merlin engine mount was steel tube with fabricated "U" support.

Cockpit entrance to Spitfire Mk. IX.

Right side cockpit view of Spitfire Mk. IX shows landing gear retraction unit, pilot stick, and windscreen de-icing system.

Early bubble type canopy on the Spitfire was beautifully streamlined.

Capt. Donald Lykins checks out Spitfire Mk. IX's cockpit prior to test flight. This was the first Spitfire to be licensed in the United States.

Spitfire MK. V b LF.

Spitfire MK. V b LF. sporting "D-Day" invasion markings. W 3560 was attached to Royal Air Force No. 132 Squadron.

Spitfire MK. 16 LF

Spitfire MK. 16 LF of the Burmese Air Force. The country of Burma purchased 30 Spitfires from the Israeli Government in 1954.

Scale: 1:48

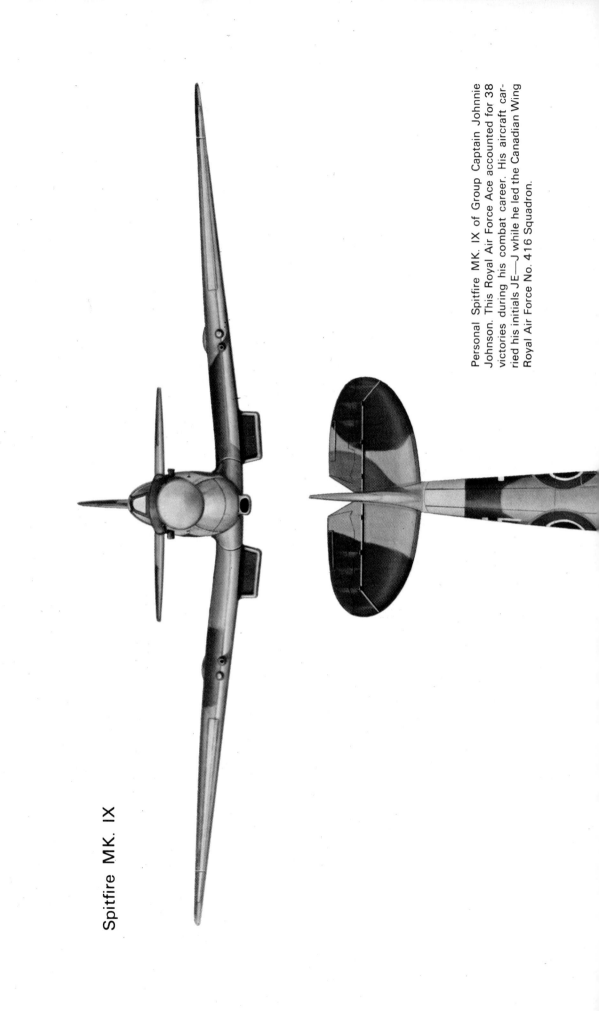

Spitfire MK. IX

Personal Spitfire MK. IX of Group Captain Johnnie Johnson. This Royal Air Force Ace accounted for 38 victories during his combat career. His aircraft carried his initials JE—J while he led the Canadian Wing Royal Air Force No. 416 Squadron.

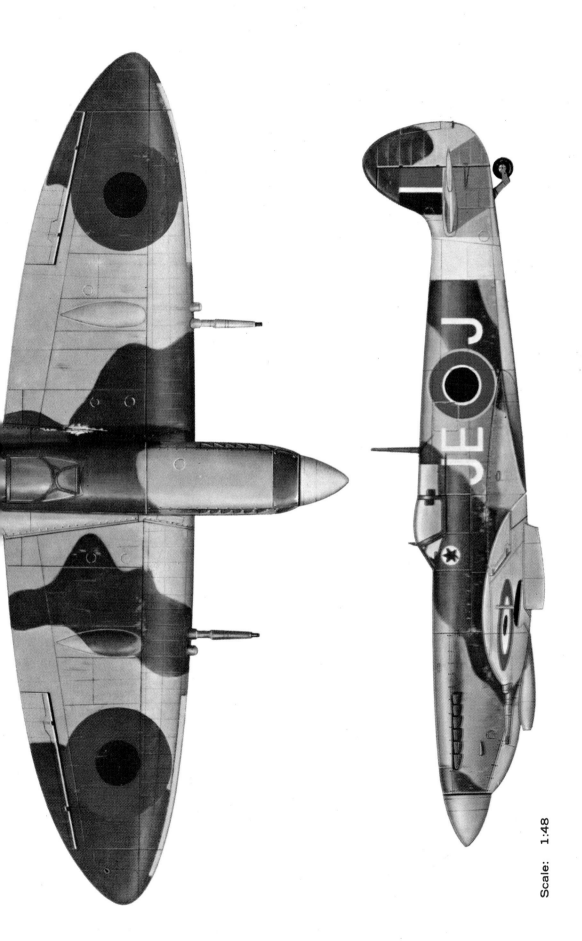

Scale: 1:48

Spitfire MK. V b

Spitfire MK. V b of the Turkish Air Force was a gift to Turkey in 1943 by the British Government. They flew alongside Turkish FW-190's in Squadron service.

Captured Spitfire MK. II b. Shot down over France. This Spitfire was repaired by Luftwaffe mechanics and test flown by German pilots.

Spitfire MK. II b.

Scale: 1:48

Two views of Spitfire Mk. IX's cockpit.

Left side landing gear of Spitfire Mk. IX. Landing gear was of simple design and retracted outward into wing.

Unusual view of Spitfire wing and main spar construction. Complete spar was made up by inserting component tubes into spar assembly. Outer tube is progressively reduced towards the tip, thus approaching the ultimate design.

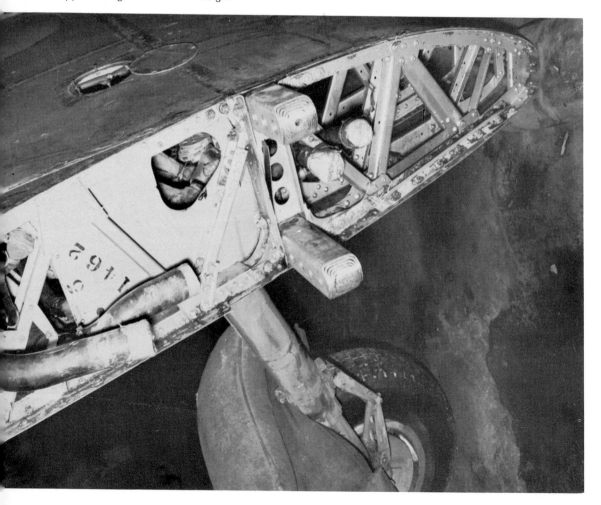

Repairing bottom side of wing on Spitfire Mk. XVI. Inspection panels and gun hatches are open to show construction details. Two small holes in R.A.F. insignia are for tie down ropes when Spitfire is parked on concrete apron.

Spitfire tail assembly was built as a unit. The rudder fin is an intregal part of the unit as two of the rear frames are extended upwards and serve as spars. Note hydraulic unit in center section for tailwheel.

Early round rudder and fin design served as a distinguishing identification on all early model Spitfires. Tail wheel of the Spitfire Mk. IX was non-retractable.

Spitfire Mk. IX movable tail surfaces were of metal construction but were fabric covered. No ball bearings were used in Spitfire movable hinge controls. Simple brass bushings served this purpose and were expended when badly worn. Note both elevators had trim tabs to counter torque from engine.

Supermarine Spitfire Mk. XVI TE-330 now on display at the Air Force Museum, Dayton, Ohio. This aircraft was a gift of the Royal Air Force to the U.S. Air Force Academy. Japanese Kawanishi "George 21" fighter in the background.

Side view of U.S. Air Force Museum's Spitfire Mk. XVI. This model was a basic Mark IX model fitted with a bubble canopy and an American built Packard Merlin engine.

Flight of Seafire Mk. Ib's on escort duties. The first Seafires for the Royal Navy were converted R.A.F. Spitfire Mk. V's.

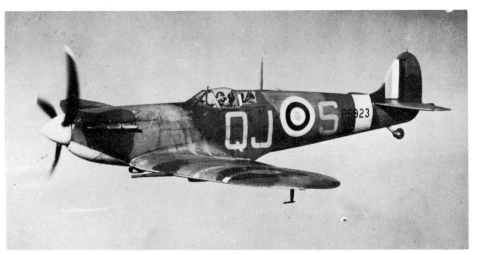

Supermarine Spitfire Mk. Vb R-6923 was a presentation aircraft. One of many purchased by India and given to the Royal Air Force during World War II. This one belonged to the East India Squadron.

Flight of six Spitfire Mk. II's of R.A.F. Fighter Squadron No. 65 on the prowl. This famous squadron saw considerable action in the early air battles over Britain.

This Spitfire Mk. VII EN-474 was sent to the United States by the R.A.F. in early 1943. It was tested by the Army Air Force at Wright Field. This model was a high altitude fighter. Note the long pointed wing tips.

Standard production model in the famous series was the Spitfire MK. IX seen here fitted with a 90 gallon slipper tank. 5,665 Spitfire Mk. IX's were built during WW II.

Spitfire pilot takes time out to watch a local "pub" attendant transfer keg of beer into special "joy juice" tank to be flown to front line British troops in Normandy. Note the "D-Day" invasion markings on this Spitfire Mk. IX wing undersides.

Royal Air Force Spitfire Mk. XIV on a Normandy Beach Head air strip a few days after "D-Day". Pilot was forced to land when he ran short of fuel on fighter sweep to Southern France. U.S. 56th Fighter Group P-47 Thunderbolts are in background. Metal matting served as temporary runway for most early beach head air strips.

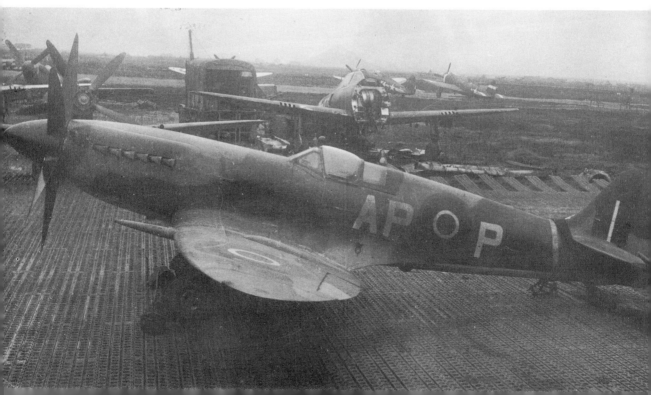

A Spitfire Mk. I prepares to take off from a forward airfield near channel to intercept oncoming Luftwaffe bombers. When the first Mark I's were introduced to R.A.F. service they were fitted with fixed pitch wood propellers. They were later replaced by De Havilland controllable pitch propellers and this greatly improved take off and climb characteristics.

Spitfire Mk. VII had just landed for repairs at St. Mer-Eglese, France. This aircraft was based at Calmshed, England and was forced to land after "Ramrod Mission" to Bordeaux, France on 13 August 1944. Note aircraft still bears "D-Day" invasion markings on bottom of wing.

By early 1942 most all "Battle of Britain" Spitfires had been replaced by later models. This Spitfire Mk. I R-7143 was a favorite of a R.A.F. Squadron and was retained as a joy ride aircraft for the pilot's pleasure. Note camouflage has been stripped off and guns have been removed.

The Army Air Force took charge of a number of Spitfire aircraft like this Mk. Vb AR-372. It was named "The Sad Sack", by the pilots that flew it. Pilot in cockpit was Capt. Boardman Reed. This Spitfire belonged to the 14th Photo-Recon Squadron, 7th Photo-Recon. Group; 8th Air Force based at Mt. Farm, Oxford, England.

One of the famous Eagle Squadron Spitfire Mk. Vb aircraft at rest while part of the Biggin Hill Wing. The Eagle Squadron was composed of volunteer American pilots who flew for the R.A.F. prior to the entry of the United States into World War II.

Spitfire Mk. VIII SF-447 as used in North Africa were tropicalized and sent immediately overseas from production centers in England.

A Western Desert Spitfire Mk. Vc BR-390 at an American air base in Lybia.

Army Air Force Spitfire P.R. XI PA-892 was an adaption of the basic Mark IX for photographic work.

This Supermarine Spitfire P.R. 19 PM-631 is still active and is seen here at R.A.F. Station Coltishall. The P.R. 19 was the final photo-recon. version of the Spitfire series.

An Irish Air Corps Spitfire Mk. IX Trainer was formerly R.A.F. TE-308. This aircraft was delivered in 1951 to the Irish Air Corps with five other Spitfire Mk. IX two place trainers. Rear cockpit was fitted with bubble type sliding canopy.

This Irish Air Corps Spitfire Mk. IX Trainer was modified from a standard R.A.F. Spitfire fighter after W.W. II.

A late production Spitfire Mk. 22 on the flight ramp at R.A.F. Station Cottesmore. A new wing design was fitted and the Spitfire lost its characteristic elliptical form. This new wing was made stronger than earlier models. It carried four 20mm Hispano Cannon. The Rolls Royce Griffon 61 or 65 engine was used, driving a five blade Rotol propeller. Top speed was 450 m.p.h. at 19,000 feet.

Spitfire Mk. IX at Biggin Hill as used in the film "The Longest Day."

The first Griffon engine Spitfire was the Mark XII.

This Seafire Mk. XV PR-434 was one that saw service with the Royal Canadian Navy.

This Spitfire Mk. 24 VN-318 was the last of the Spitfire line. These aircraft were built in 1946 and were finally retired from the Royal Air Force in 1952. A few remain as gate memorials at several R.A.F. Air Stations.

Close in flight view of Spitfire Mk. 21. Production of this model commenced in the fall of 1944 and lasted until early 1946. Only 120 were built.

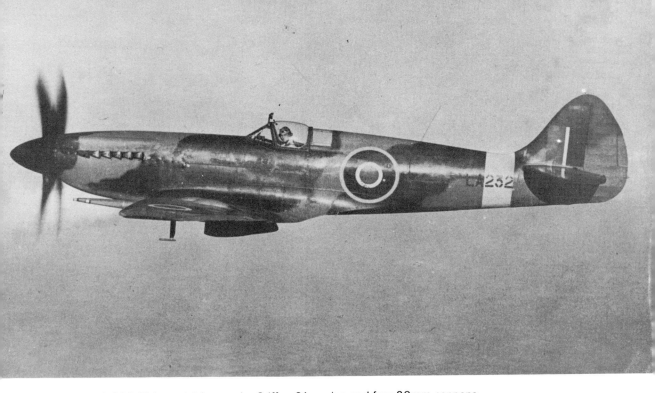

Spitfire Mk. 21 LA-232. This model featured a Griffon 61 engine and four 20mm cannons.

Supermarine Spitfire Mk. 22 PK-312 flies above the English countryside. It saw service with the R.A.F. at Malta until 1948.

Flight view of the first Griffon powered Spitfire, the Mark XII. Only 100 of these fighters were built. It successfully proved the adaptation of the new Griffon engine to a Spitfire airframe.

The Spitfire Mk. XII was built as an answer to the fast Focke-Wulf 190's which were making repeated "hit and run" raids on the south coast of England. Armament was two 20mm cannon and four .303 Browning machine guns.

Above the blue skies of England this unusual view of a Spitfire shows a "wing over" maneuver by a clipped wing Mark IX. Note the 90 gallon long range slipper tank mounted below.

Spitfire Mk. VIII two seat trainer in British Civil Markings G-AIDN .

Carrier take off of a Seafire Mk. IIc with the assistance of R.A.T.O.G.-Rocket Assist take off rocket.

This Royal Air Force Spitful RB-515 was the first production model of a new series. It was completed in early 1945 as a replacement for Spitfire aircraft. It featured a revised wing platform and a laminar flow wing. It had a large rudder and was powered by a Griffon 69 engine.

This Seafang prototype RB-520 was a standard R.A.F. Spiteful fighter with the addition of carrier hook for use by the Royal Navy.

Supermarine Seafire Mk. 46 of the Royal Navy. This model was the last of the Seafire series. It used the counter-rotating Griffon 87 engine driving two 3-bladed propellers. Maximum speed was 450 m.p.h. at 20,000 feet.

Ground view of Royal Navy Seafire Mk. 47. Armament carried was four 20mm Hispano Cannon. Note counter-rotating propellers.

Royal Canadian Navy Seafire Mk. XV SR-464 was one that saw active service aboard a Canadian aircraft carrier following World War II.

A Canadian civil Spitfire CF-NUS was formerly a clipped wing Mark IX. It was used for several years by the Belgium firm C.O.G.E.A. for towing targets for the Belgium Air Force. Later it was sold to a Canadian businessman and imported to Canada. Today, it is one of three Spitfire fighters held by the Canadian National Aviation Museum.

A Royal Air Force Spitfire P.R.19 on static display at Farnborough, England. These high speed photo-recon. aircraft did not carry armament. They were used late in the war to bring back information for advancing Allied Armies in Europe.

Spitfire Mk. 1 K-9942 Coded RN-V is used by the British Air Ministry as a display aircraft and is shown here at a London "Battle of Britain" display.

Spitfire Mk. I at Whitehall. London, England for annual "Battle of Britain" display. Note Luftwaffe Junkers 88 and Bf-109E in background.

Team mate of the Spitfire during the hectic days of the "Battle of Britain" was the R.A.F. Hawker Hurricane. This Hurricane IIc LF-363 is one of the few remaining Hurricanes preserved by the R.A.F. and can be seen today at R.A.F. Station, Coltishal, England.

Line up of Historic Fighters of the Past at R.A.F. Station, Colerne. Spitfire Mk. II P-7350, Auster Spotter WE-600, Hawker Hunter, Messerschmitt Me-163 B "Komet", Meteor, Heinkel He-162A, and Gloster "Javelin."

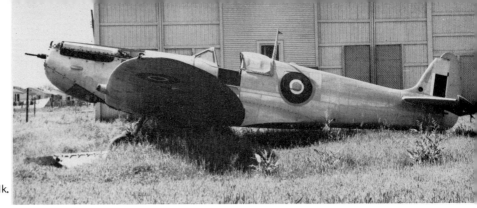

A former Royal Navy Seafire Mk. IIc in the United States.

This ex-Royal Air Force Spitfire Mk. XIV TZ-138 was sent to Canada for Cold Winter Tests during 1946-47.

This Spitfire Mk. XIV was entered n the National Air Races at Cleve-and in 1949. It placed 3rd. in the Tinnerman Trophy Race. It bore race number eighty.

Last days of a Royal Navy Seafire Mk. XV 5X280. This aircraft was one of many on a Naval dump awaiting the scrapman's axe.

MODEL	POWER PLANT	MAX. SPEED	RANGE	CRUISING SPEED	SERVICE CEILING	ARMAMENT	SPAN, FT	LENGTH	HEIGHT	WT. EMPTY	GROSS WEIGHT
Spitfire IA	Rolls-Royce Merlin III 12-cylinder, 1030 hp.	357 mph at 19,000 ft	575 mls	315 mph 20,000 ft	34,000 ft	8x0.303 in. Browning MG	36 ft 10 in.	29 ft 11 in.	11 ft 5 in.	4810 lb	5784 lb
Spitfire VC	Rolls-Royce Merlin 45 12-cylinder, 1470 hp.	374 mph at 13,000 ft	470 mls int. fuel	322 mph 20,000 ft	37,000 ft	2x20 mm Hispano cannons 4x0.303 in. MG	36 ft 10 in.	29 ft 11 in.	11 ft 5 in.	5100 lb	6785 lb
Spitfire VI	Rolls-Royce Merlin 47 12 cylinder, 1415 hp.	364 mph at 22,000 ft	510 mls int. fuel	325 mph 20,000 ft	40,000 ft	2x20 mm Hispano cannons 4x0.303 in. MG	40 ft 2 in.	30 ft 2 in.	11 ft 5 in.	5300 lb	7178 lb
Spitfire VII	Rolls-Royce Merlin 64 12 cylinder, 1710 hp.	408 mph at 25,000 ft	660 mls int. fuel	324 mph 20,000 ft	43,000 ft	2x20 mm Hispano cannons 4x0.303 in. MG	40 ft 2 in.	31 ft 3 in.	12 ft 7 in.	6000 lb	7875 lb
Spitfire F VIII	Rolls-Royce Merlin 63 12 cylinder	408 mph at 25,000 ft	660 mls int. fuel	324 mph 20,000 ft	43,000 ft	2x20 mm Hispano cannons, 4x0.303 in. MG or 4x20 mm cannons plus 1x500 lb, 2x250 lb bombs	36 ft 10 in.	31 ft 3 in.	12 ft 7 in.	5800 lb	7767 lb
Spitfire L.F. IXE	Rolls-Royce Merlin 66 12-cylinder, 1720 hp.	404 mph at 21,000 ft	434 mls int. fuel	328 mph 20,000 ft	42,500 ft	2x20 mm Hisp. can., 2x0.5 in. Browning MG 1x500 lb, 2x250 lb bombs	32 ft 7 in.	31 ft 4 in.	12 ft 7 in.	5800 lb	7500 lb
Spitfire XII	Rolls-Royce Griffon III 65 12-cylinder, 1735 hp.	393 mph at 18,000 ft	329 mls int. fuel	364 mph 20,000 ft	44,000 ft	2x20 mm Hispano cannons 4x0.303 in. Browning MG	32 ft 7 in.	31 ft 10 in.	11 ft 0 in.	5600 lb	7400 lb
Spitfire Mk. 21	Rolls-Royce Griffon 61 12 cylinder, 2050 hp.	420 mph at 20,000 ft	490 mls int. fuel	385 mph 20,000 ft	43,500 ft	4x20 mm Hispano Mk II cannons 1x500 lb, 2x250 lb bombs	36 ft 11 in.	32 ft. 8 in.	13 ft 6 in.	6900 lb	9200 lb
Seafire Mk. III	Rolls-Royce Merlin 55 12-cylinder, 1470 hp.	352 mph at 12,250 ft	465 mls int. fuel	310 mph 20,000 ft	33,800 ft	2x20 mm Hispano cannons 4x0.303 Browning MG 1x500 lb, 2x250 lb bombs	36 ft 10 in.	30 ft 2 in.	11 ft 2 in.	5400 lb	7100 lb
Spiteful F. XIV	Rolls-Royce Griffon 69 12 cylinder, 2375 hp.	483 mph at 26,000 ft	564 mls int. fuel	385 mph 20,000 ft	42,000 ft	4x20 mm Hispano Mk V cannons	35 ft 0 in.	32 ft 11 in.	13 ft 5 in.	7350 lb	9950 lb

THE SEAFIRE

During 1941 German U-Boat successes in the Atlantic were widespread. The sealanes were no safe haven for Allied vessels once they were out of protective range of shore base patrol planes.

Long range Focke-Wulf 200 "Condor" Bombers hit unprotected convoys out at sea. The need arose for a fighter to protect these vital convoys to England and Russia.

The first development was the catapult Hurricanes from C.A.M. ships. Later this gave way to escort carriers. A decision was made to modify existing aircraft types for fleet duty. Both the Spitfire and Hurricane were selected and this was the first time a tradition in naval aircraft was broken. Prior to this time, the old belief that navy fighters were inferior to contemporary land-based fighters was due to the fact that the British Admiralty specifications called for fighters which were generally slow, large, and had to be multi-purpose aircraft.

The prototype Seafire was a standard Spitfire VB fitted with a carrier hook. The production Seafire MK. 1Bs were standard Spitfire MK. VB airframes fitted with arrester hooks and catapult gear for assisted takeoff. The need was urgent, and many Seafires were produced on the production lines by modifying existing Spitfire V's.

No provisions were made for folding wings on the early Seafires. They had to remain on the decks of the small escort carriers at all times.

This made servicing quite difficult, and the exposure to rough seas was constant and with the risk of damage. Only a limited number could be accommodated on the deck of each carrier.

The Seafire II was similar to the MK. I except for the fitting of the MK. Vc universal wing armament. A number of Seafire MK. II's were fitted with cameras for photo-recon missions and these were designated P.R. Seafires MK. III.

With the introduction of the Seafire MK. III the disadvantage of the fixed wing gave way to the folding wing. This version acquired the nickname "Praying Mantis" by its wing folding appearance. The wings were folded manually and were supported by jury struts.

With the introduction of the new Griffon engine the Seafire Series grew in performance. The Seafire MK. XV gave the Royal Navy a top ranking carrier fighter. It was more than a match for any Axis fighter. As a development of the Seafire MK. III, it was a basic sea version of the Spitfire XII which was a proven land based fighter. The added five hundred horsepower of the Griffon engine resulted in improved rate of climb and top speed. The Seafire XV was built by the Westland Aircraft Company.

The Seafire MK. XVII was an improved version of the MK. VX. A stronger landing gear was fitted to take the hard carrier landings. A bubble type canopy was fitted to improve visibility. Provisions were also made for "RATO." (Rocket assisted take off.)

The Seafire MK. XVIII employed the 1890 h.p. Griffon Model 36 engine. It was proposed to supersede the Seafire MK. XVII just as soon as the Model 36 Griffon engine was available. This aircraft never went into production.

The Seafire MK. 45 was a Navalised Spitfire MK. 21. It employed the 2,050 hp. Griffon Model 61 engine. It was the most powerful Seafire of the series.

The landing gear doors were modified to avoid fouling carrier arrester wires. The wings did not fold. It carried four 20 m.m. wing cannons. It had a top speed of 446 m.p.h., rate of climb was 5,300 feet per minute, service ceiling was 43,000 feet. Total production amounted to fifty aircraft.

The Seafire MK. 46 was a Navalised Spitfire MK. 22. It was not intended for quantity production and only twenty-four were built.

For the first time a 24 volt electrical system was employed. It featured a bubble canopy for better visibility and provisions were built in for "RATO," and rockets could be fitted to the wing undersides.

Considerable torque was experienced with the five blade Rotol propeller and so a six blade counter-rotating propeller was fitted, which eliminated this problem.

The Seafire MK. 47 was the final development in the long line of Seafires. It featured a folding wing, but unlike the earlier Seafire MK. III, each wing folded upward as a unit. The last Seafire MK. 47 came off the production line in March of 1949. It had a top speed of 451 m.p.h. rate of climb 5,200 feet per minute, range of 930 miles and a service ceiling of 41,200 feet. Wing armament was four 20 m.m. cannons.

This model Seafire saw service in Malaya in 1949 and also operated off the H.M.S. Triumph, 1950, during the Korean Conflict.

The Seafang was a Navalised version of the Spiteful and was a relative of the Spitfire Series, but was not similar in appearance. The wing shape was changed and only ten Seafangs were manufactured before production ended. It had a top speed of 475 m.p.h., rate of climb 4,100 feet per minute, service ceiling of 32,000 feet and a normal range of 735 miles. A total of 2,408 Seafires have been produced.

THE SPEED SPITFIRE

A special racing version of the Spitfire was built during 1938 for an attempt on the world's land plane speed record. This aircraft became known as the "Speed Spitfire."

The current record stood at 352 m.p.h. which was held by Howard Hughes. A decision was made to abandon the attempt after the noted German flyer·Ernest Udet set a record of 394 m.p.h. in a special Heinkel 112U.

The Speed Spitfire was a basic production Spitfire. Its powerful Rolls Royce Merlin engine was specially supercharged to give top performance. It drove a three bladed all metal De Havilland propeller.

The notable difference in the Speed Spitfire from contemporary Spitfires was the smooth contoured windshield. Although it was never used for a speed record attempt, the Speed Spitfire was fifty miles faster than standard production Spitfires. It was used to gather high-speed flight and research data.

When the German Army invaded Norway in 1940, a need for a high speed fighter to operate from Norwegian fjords and lakes was paramount. Preparations were put into effect to produce a floatplane version of the Spitfire. Norway fell to the advancing German Army before production could commence and so only a few prototype models were made.

ONTARIO AIR MUSEUM'S SPITFIRE MK. 19

In the summer of 1959 King Bhumibol of Thailand and his lovely family visited the United States. During their stay, the Royal Family visited The Air Museum then located in Claremont, California. They were impressed with what they saw.

King Bhomibol maintained his own private Air Museum in Bangkok, Thailand. Upon his return to Thailand the King made a gift of a Spitfire MK. 19 to the Ontario Air Museum. Its condition was unknown at the time the gift was accepted. Approximately two years later this Spitfire was shipped to the United States, via Bob Prescott and the Flying Tiger Air Line. The aircraft arrived at Burbank, California in 1962 and passed through customs.

Walker Mahurin, a Deputy Director for Space Systems Division of North American Aviation volunteered to tackle the job of restoration. The propeller was sent to the Rotol factory in England for overhaul. The Rotol people did an excellent job on the propeller and it is in new condition. The Rolls Royce "Griffon" engine was then crated and shipped to the factory in England. However the engine had seen considerable service and it is not repairable. If a Griffon Model 65 or comparable engine can be found the aircraft will be made flyable; however the picture does not look too bright as no spare Griffon engine has been found in the search of the past three years.

The Ontario Air Museums Spitfire MK. 19 was one of 225 production machines built by Vickers-Armstrong in the role of high speed photo-recon duties. It was Coded PS-890 by the Royal Air Force and saw service in the Far East.

In 1947 it was stationed in Malaya and was attached to No. 81 Squadron R.A.F. It was used for photo-recon missions against Communist bandit camps in operations throughout Malaya. It continued in R.A.F. service all during the Korean War.

In the late fifties it was sold together with a number of Spitfire MK. XIV E's to the Thailand Air Force. Modern jet fighters had replaced it in the Royal Air Force.

If a Griffon engine can be located, perhaps it too can be added to the flying aircraft display of the Ontario Air Museum.

Volume 12

The Heinkel He 100

Also revealing the true story
behind the He-113 Luftwaffe
Mystery fighter

52 pages 4 color page

Volume 11

The CHANCE VOUGHT "Corsair"

52 pages   4 color pages

Volume 13

The HEINKEL He 177 "Greif"

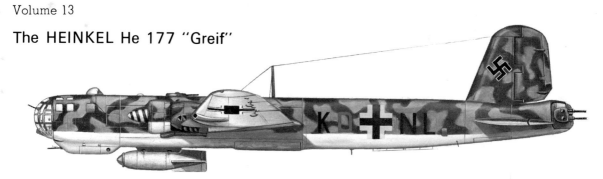

52 pages   4 color pages

a fantastic account of
Germany's only operational
Long range Bomber